Long Ago Children

By JoAnne Nelson • Pictures by John Speirs

MODERN CURRICULUM PRESS

PROJECT DIRECTOR: Judith E. Nayer
COVER DESIGN: Elaine A. Groth

Published by Modern Curriculum Press

 Modern Curriculum Press, Inc.
A division of Simon & Schuster
13900 Prospect Road, Cleveland, Ohio 44136

ISBN 0-8136-4300-7 (STY PK)   ISBN 0-8136-4296-5 (BK)

10   9   8   7   6   5   94   93   92

We moved west across the prairies.
The wagons bumped along.
At night we had a campfire
and sang our favorite song.

We built our cabin out of logs.
We worked to clear the land.
We plowed the fields and planted corn.
We did it all by hand.

Pioneer families had to grow
their own food.
There were no power machines
to help with the work.

Every day we did our chores
the very best we could.
We fed the chickens, milked the cows,
and then we chopped the wood.

Pioneer families had to make
everything they needed.
Children shared in the work
by grinding corn and
churning butter.

At first we didn't have a stove.
The fireplace gave us heat.
We cooked mush for breakfast, stew for lunch,
and POPCORN was our treat.

A kettle was hung on a pole
over an open fire.
Children helped stir the stew,
which cooked all day.

One day when all our chores were done,
we rode down to the creek.
First we had a picnic,
then we played Hide and Seek.

Pioneer children
enjoyed running races
and playing tag.
Toys were handmade
out of wood, rope,
and even corn husks.

At school we learned to do our sums.
We learned to read and write.
We did our homework by the fire
and read by lantern light.

Pioneers used lanterns or lamps.
There was no electricity.

We only took one bath each week
in a tub made out of wood.
We didn't use much water,
but oh, it felt SO GOOD!

Water was carried from rivers,
or pumped from a well.
It was heated over the fire.

At night when it was cold and dark,
we snuggled in our beds.
Grandpa told a scary story,
and we covered up our heads.

GOOD NIGHT! SLEEP TIGHT!